James Middleton Macdonald

Massilia-Carthago sacrifice tablets of the worship of Baal

Reproduced in facsimile, edited, translated and compared with the

Levitical Code

James Middleton MacDonald

Massilia-Carthago sacrifice tablets of the worship of Baal
Reproduced in facsimile, edited, translated and compared with the Levitical Code

ISBN/EAN: 9783337283346

Printed in Europe, USA, Canada, Australia, Japan

Cover: Foto ©Andreas Hilbeck / pixelio.de

More available books at **www.hansebooks.com**

MASSILIA-CARTHAGO

SACRIFICE TABLETS

OF THE

WORSHIP OI BAAL.

Reproduced in Facsimile, Edited, Translated, and Compared with the Levitical Code,

BY

THE REVEREND

JAMES MIDDLETON MACDONALD, M.A.,

Houghton Syriac Prizeman, Oxford.

𝔏onbon :

D. NUTT, 270–271, STRAND,

1897.

INTRODUCTION.

THE Massilia Sacrifice-Tablet shows in its first two words that it was intended for use in the worship of Baal; and as we know that the Phœnicians came to Massilia from Carthage, centuries before the time of Christ, we think it quite in the eternal fitness of things that this Sacrifice-tablet should have been found in Marseilles (Massilia) in 1844; our only wonder is that the tablet remained undiscovered for 2,300 or 2,400 years.

The doubts and disputes about the stone itself have all faded into oblivion; but before passing on to the inscription on the stone, we may as well sketch the later history of the stone.

At the close of the year 1844, a workman happened to be repairing the wall of a house in Marseilles which stood at that time almost on the ground of what is now the Sanctuary of the new Cathedral close to the quay. The workman mentioned to his employer and to the landlord that there was curious writing on one of the stones.

On examination it was found that there were two large pieces of one tablet, and unfortunately the left piece was chipped along the lower half.

A 2

Were such a stone found nowadays, everyone would at once be on his guard against forgery; but in the fifth decade of our century scholars' faith in finding had not been rudely shaken by Shapira, so the fact that the subject-matter on the stone was akin to the Levitical laws of sacrifice, did not deter scholars from thinking out the Massilia sacrifice-tablet on its merits.

When the "find" was announced, prudent investigators in epigraphy were divided into two classes.

a. Those who said that there was an ancient Pagan temple on the seashore on a spot which is now beneath the sea-level, but that this temple was probably devoted to the worship of Diana; and furthermore that the stone on which the inscription is engraved looks as if it were composed of the same materials as those in the rocks near Marseilles.

b. Those who based their argument on the fact that the inscription is Phœnician with Carthaginian names therein, and that the Phœnician sailors and resident merchants were certain to have a Temple of Baal.

Patient investigation showed that the *b* argument led in the right direction ; for a chemical analysis of a fragment of the Massilia-tablet showed that its constituents are not those of the rocks around Marseilles, but that they are absolutely identical with those of the rocks close to Carthage, a fact proved by comparing the fragment of the Massilia-tablet with a chip from a tablet in the Louvre which was brought direct from Carthage. The Massilia-tablet is now deposited in the Museum at Marseilles, and should be an object of historic pride to the good people of Marseilles; but, as a matter of fact, they know nothing about it.

From the point of view of comparative philology

it was most fortunate that Mr. Nathan Davis discovered a similar but shorter sacrifice-tablet for Baal-worshippers in Carthage itself,* during his investigations there in 1858, and, after reading them both, we can at once see that there was a sacrificial code in Carthage compiled by authority, in much the same way as the Levitical code was drawn up by authority for use in the worship of Jehovah.

The purpose of the Massilia-tablet is manifest, viz., that the Phœnician colonists and careless sailors might know at first hand what were the proper dues to be paid to the priest in the sacrificial worship of Baal. In both the Massilia and Carthago-tablets the priests and the laity have their rights, privileges, responsibilities and punishments. The pious poor are carefully protected from rapacious priests.

The tone of both these sacrifice-tablets is simple and pure, resembling the simple code which Moses promulgated by Divine command in the wilderness, rather than the elaborate Levitical code drawn up by the priestly caste for the nation of Israel at a much later date when the priests ruled the nation.

The Massilia sacrifice-tablet is promulgated by order of (⊙)𐤉𐤔𐤀𐤋𐤏𐤂𐤓𐤋𐤄 Ḥalaṭsbaal the judge, just as the first code for the nation of Israel was issued by Moses the chief civil authority. The Massilia-tablet lets in a flood of light on the proneness of the Hebrews to drift towards the worship of Baal.

Judges ii, 13.   וַיַּעַזְבוּ אֶת־יְהוָֹה וַיַּעַבְדוּ לַבָּעַל

הוֹצֵא אֶת־בִּנְךָ וְיָמֹת כִּי נָתַץ אֶת־מִזְבַּח הַבַּעַל
Judges vi, 30.

* Known as the Carthago-tablet.

וַיְהִי כַּאֲשֶׁר מֵת גִּדְעוֹן וַיָּשׁוּבוּ בְּנֵי יִשְׂרָאֵל וַיִּזְנוּ אַחֲרֵי

הַבְּעָלִים וַיָּשִׂימוּ לָהֶם בַּעַל בְּרִית לֵאלֹהִים

Judges viii, 33.

1 Kings, xvi, 32.   וַיָּקֶם מִזְבֵּחַ לַבַּעַל בֵּית הַבַּעַל

and the Massilia-tablet shows how easy it would be
for time-serving priests and prophets of Jehovah to
become priests and prophets of Baal in the time of
Jezebel, when the Baal-cult became the Court religion.

וַיֹּאמֶר אֵלִיָּהוּ אֶל־הָעָם אֲנִי נוֹתַרְתִּי נָבִיא לַיהוָה

לְבַדִּי וּנְבִיאֵי הַבַּעַל אַרְבַּע מֵאוֹת וַחֲמִשִּׁים אִישׁ

1 Kings xviii, 22.

As aforesaid, there are differences between the
simple Baal-code and the detailed code of Jehovah's
worship in the Book of Leviticus; but the resem-
blances are so striking that we must, for the purposes
of this thesis, put aside theories of inspiration, plenary
or otherwise; and must consider them as sister codes
of sister nations, both nations speaking the same
language with but slight dialectic differences.

The Phœnician sailor who sailed from Massilia to
Tyre could read the Levitical parchments in the
Hebrew synagogue at Jaffa; and, if he went inland
for commercial reasons, he could *spell out** the inscription of Mesha the Moabite in Dibon, and then
compare them with his own tablets in his beloved
Tyre.

* If you placed Phœnician letters more to the right, and
tipped them up more horizontally, then you might fairly consider four-fifths of the Moabite alphabet like Phœnician letters.

To a degenerate Jew of the nineteenth century, reading Hebrew one day in the week, with the help of the modern Massoretic points, or perhaps only carelessly listening to a rabbi cantillating the glorious old Hebrew liturgy, the Massilia-tablet would look like Chinese; but this Phœnician character is practically the self-same character in which Jehovah with His own finger wrote the Ten Commandments, as did Moses after him. When they are discovered, as I hope that they will be, this fact will be patent to all.

When the primal pure old Hebrew character changed into Talmudic Chaldee, etc., and then into Estrangelo-Syriac, such as Jesus Christ wrote, the simpler Phœnicians retained the old character.

When the Jews were in Babylon, the study of the old primal Hebrew character was kept up by few; and as a matter of fact, when the same finger which had written the Ten Commandments on stone wrote

𐤉𐤌𐤀𐤓𐤐𐤍 𐤋𐤒𐤕 𐤀𐤍𐤌 𐤀𐤍𐤌

or as we write it now

† מנא מנא תקל ופרסין

only Daniel, the devout student of the old 𐤋𐤒𐤕 could read the oracle (even its character), pronouncing doom upon the sacrilegious Belshazzar.

---

* The ‏ي‏ is a part of the word, for even nowadays the ‏ى‏ is essential ‏فَارِسى فرسى‏.

† Professor Sayce quotes M. Clermont-Ganneau's new Aramæic attempt at a translation of this, "Reckon a maneh, a shekel and its parts," and wonders why the wise men of Babylon who understood Aramæic could not read the oracle. I still say that the hand of God wrote the words in the archaic Semitic character.

who had toasted Bel and Nebo in the sacrificial chalices of Jehovah's worship taken from the Temple in Jerusalem.

Anyone studying Hebrew in the present character must remember that the oldest manuscript of the Old Testament is 1400 years later than our Massilia-tablet, and 1800 years later than Mesha's inscription on the Moabite Stone.

With regard to Baal-worship, it was probably the same throughout the littoral of the Mediterranean.

With a little imagination we can form a picture of the service in a good 𐤋𐤏𐤂𐤓𐤀, taking as the working sketch for our picture the scenes in 2 Kings x, 20–27, where the cathedral of Baal in Samaria was full of earnest Baal-devotees from the altar to the door פֶּה לָפֶה,* so full that their mouths almost touched each other.

The grandeur of the vestments reminds us of the vestments (לְבוּשׁ) appertaining to the house of Aaron; but in the Baal-cult every *layman* donned a grand robe while in the presence of the mighty god.

The sacrifices זְבָחִים וְעֹלוֹת (and especially the burnt-offering) were almost the same as in the Hebrew Temple to Jehovah in Jerusalem; but the *stone statues* (אֶת־מַצְּבוֹת בֵּית הַבַּעַל)† to 𐤋𐤏𐤂𐤓𐤀

---

* It is an assumption of the Revised Version of the Old Testament that פֶּה לָפֶה means *from* one end to the other.

† The Revised Version of the Old Testament studiously translates מַצֵּבָה by "pillar" or "obelisk"; but the context of several passages and the conjunction and antithesis of אֲשֵׁרָה, the female carved goddess, lead me to think that the מַצְבֹת

Baal Berith, 𐤋𐤏𐤁 Ḥamōn, 𐤆𐤁𐤁 Zebūb, 𐤐𐤏𐤓 Peōr.

𐤑𐤐𐤍 Tsephōn, erected along the side walls are non-Hebraic, though essentially Phœnician. They are quite distinct from the great image of the local Baal

(אֶת מַצֶּבַת הַבַּעַל) which was at the inner end of the temple.

Let us examine the inscription on the Massilia-tablet letter by letter, and of necessity in the original photograph; for the type which is supplied to us as Phœnician is at times ludicrously unlike the same letters as shown in the photograph. Wherever a restoration has been effected in a hiatus, the same has been given in the original Phœnician.

The learned scholar who wrote the monograph on the Massilia-tablet in the *Corpus Inscriptionum* (Paris) for the French Academy, restored the lost phrase or word *in Hebrew and Latin* but not in Phœnician.

I think that this was a mistake, and I have therefore given what I believe to be the original Phœnician.

In one or two places I differ from the above writer.

were male gods in stone ranged *inside*, down the side walls of the Cathedral of Baal.

Take a single passage conjoining carved female and carved male gods :

כִּי אֶת־מִזְבְּחֹתָם תִּתֹּצוּן וְאֶת מַצֵּבֹתָם תְּשַׁבֵּרוּן וְאֶת־
אֲשֵׁרָיו תִּכְרֹתוּן   Exodus xxxiv, 13.

The *stone pillars were outside* the cathedral.

I have a photograph of the finest sun pillar in India. It was originally outside the Sun Temple at Kanārak, but was brought by the Lion dynasty to the Lion-Gate of the Jagannath (Juggernaut) Temple in Puri.

There is never more that one such pillar, and it is always *outside* the temple.

The מַצֵּבוֹת 𐤌𐤑𐤁𐤕 were many and were inside, for Jehu ordered them *to be brought out*.

after having scrutinised the injured spot with a magnifying glass.

Line 1 :—

ᚠᚮᚦᚦ[. . . .]ᚤᚮᚹ×ᚦᚦ[. . . .]ᚦ]ᚮᚷ [. . . .]᚜ᚮᚷᚦᚷ

ᚖᚤᚹᚱ]ᚪᚷᚤᚷ ᚦᚤᚦᚪᚷᚤᚷ ᚖᚤᚹᚱ ᚜ᚮᚷ [. . . .]

] ᚔᚤ ᚜ᚮᚷᚱ᚜ᚔᚤᚷ ᚤᚤᚹ×ᚪᚷ ᚤᚷ

The phrase ᚜ᚮᚷᚦᚷ at once stamps the inscription as a religious document of the Baal-cult, but it is exasperating that the stone should have been injured just at the name of the local Baal.

Take a magnifying glass and look at the injured spot, and observe the remaining tails of three letters all below the line. The first tail points to the right, and the other two bend towards the left.

On examining any large number of Phœnician tablets in the British Museum, The Louvre, etc., it will be seen that a very common Baal in Africa is ᚤᚤᚔ᚜ᚮᚷ.

The second and third tails might pass for those of ᚤᚤ, but there is only one tail for the first letter. It is almost certain that the first letter had only one tail; the name that at once occurs is ᚤᚱᚱ᚜ᚮᚷ. The tail of the first letter exactly corresponds with that of ᚱ and that of the second is much more like ᚱ than ᚤ.

The above argument shuts out ᚤᚤᚔ as well as ᚤᚤᚔ. Gen. xxxvi, 38, 39.

If one could disbelieve the evidence of the eye, then ᚤᚤᚔ would be a charming restoration, but we must prefer 𐤁𐤏𐤋𐤑𐤐𐤍. The name occurs as a place in Exodus xiv, 2, 9, לִפְנֵי בַּעַל צְפֹן, and also in slightly different Hebrew in Numb. xxxiii, 7, אֲשֶׁר עַל־פְּנֵי בַּעַל צְפוֹן both passages have the antique essence of a name in being topographical.

𐤁𐤏𐤋𐤑𐤐𐤍 would seem to mean the god of "hidden knowledge," but it may mean the great god of " The North."

The North was the region of religious mystery. Lucifer sat in the North.   Evil came from the North. The King of Kings came from the North.

הִנְנִי מֵבִיא אֶל־צֹר נְבוּכַדְרָאצַּר מֶלֶךְ־בָּבֶל מִצָּפוֹן מֶלֶךְ מְלָכִים. Ezek. xxvi, 7.

𐤑𐤐𐤍 عبد was a Phœnician name in Africa like عبدالله among Mussulmans, so that 𐤑𐤐𐤍 is not a harsh restoration.

— — — — —

[𐤕𐤕𐤗𐤔𐤅𐤄𐤂𐤕]𐤏𐤍 is a certain restoration, for we luckily find both words complete in Mr. Nathan Davis's tablet in the British Museum, which tablet he found in Carthage itself.

Hebrew usage would at once lead us to translate 𐤏𐤕 "in the time of";* but we see later on in this self-same line that the genius of Phœnician employs 𐤏𐤕 "time" *without a preposition.*

𐤏𐤕 is therefore a noun.

* Compare 𐤆𐤉𐤆𐤏 in the Moabite Stone.

I am not quite sure; but from the fact that בְּעָה, a good Hebrew word, seems to be of the same sound, and from a comparison of other words in our tablet, I incline to the view that the Phœnician final ﬤ was often pronounced like ﻞ, just as it is in Arabic. Arabic writes the ﺓ *e.g.*, دَوْلَة, but pronounces it daulah د, مَدْرَسَة is pronounced madraseh; Syriac ܡܕܪܫܬܐ gives the final ܠ and then adds ܐ for euphony.

Aramæic later words derived from בְּעָה would suggest "the *demand*" of the taxes. St. Luke, xii, 45,

ܘܢܫܪܐ ܠܡܐܟܠ ܘܠܡܫܬܐ:

ܙܒܝܢ means "the *sale*" of the taxes;* the context, however, would cause us to translate freely "the *list*" of the taxes. ﲄﴯﭏﺎ. We get the singular מַשְּׂאַת ﭏﺎﴯ in 2 Chron. xxiv, 6, אֶת־מַשְׂאַת מֹשֶׁה meaning the temple-tax imposed by authority, and with the weight of ages helping it; there it means "a proper burden," here we take it as "the taxes," ﲄ]﴾ﵰﴯ.

ﵰﴯ is good Phœnician for אֲשֶׁר; Aramæic sometimes had only שׁ. It is thought that שִׁילֹה is the best reading of Gen. xlix, 10, and that the Septuagint expresses the meaning in the expanded τὰ ἀποκείμενα αὐτῷ.

ﲄ]﴾ﵰ Again we are fortunate enough to find the entire word in Davis's Carthago-tablet.

* The *Corpus Inscriptionum* says بَيْعَة, but it is not usual Arabic.

𝓕𝓕𝔁𝔀𝔂𝟹 𝓛o 𝔀𝔁 𝔂𝔀𝔁𝟹 is a restoration which is offered, because it occurs in so many words in an inscription in the British Museum, known by the name of the depositor, The Revd. J. Fenner. Note that the final two 𝓕𝓕 still remain in our inscription, making the restoration a moral certainty.

𝓛o is good old Semitic for being set over, in charge of anything.

עַל־הַנִּצָּבִים, 1 Kings iv, 5, " over the officers."

𝓛o𝟿[ר𝓛𝟹]𝓕o. From line 19 we get the missing letters.

* ⊙𝟽𝔀𝟹 Halatsbaal was not only a temple ruler, he was the renowned chief civil authority or judge. On some private votive tablets in the Public Library of Paris we see such titles as ⊙𝟽𝔀𝟹, *e.g.*, 𝔂𝓛𝔁𝟿𝓛𝝠 = barber of the gods, The Temple-barber.

Halatsbaal was the son of Bodtanet and grandson of Bodesmun 𝟾𝔂𝔀𝔁𝗮𝟿𝟾𝗼𝓕𝟾𝓕𝗮𝟿𝟾.

Line 2 :—

𝓛o𝟿ר 𝓛ⓐ𝟿𝟿 𝟾 𝔂𝔀𝔁𝗮𝟿𝟾𝟿 ⊙𝟽 𝔀𝟹[𝓛o𝟿 ר𝓛ⓐ𝟺
[𝔂𝟾𝗮𝟿] ⓐ𝟺

His colleague was another Halatsbaal, also a civil judge. He is the man mentioned in line 19 as son of Bodesmun. It would appear as if these officers of rank were uncle and nephew, the one being son and the other being grandson of the great Bodesmun.

* Livy invariably translates ⊙𝟽𝔀𝟹 "the chief civil authority," among the Carthaginians. Livy, xxviii, 37, transliterating it as Sufes. Ignorance of its Semitic origin caused the *f* to be doubled (Suffes) later on.

After this genealogical tree comes ɥⳑꝗⳆꝖᗺ as we may assert, seeing that it occurs after the same tree in line 19.

The word must mean " and their colleagues."

Fenner's inscription tells of ten such temple-officials in Carthage ɥⳁꭓᗺⳆꝗᗻꝈꝺ.

It is quite a Semitic word, for we have חָבֵר Ps. cxix, 63, חֲבֶרֶת Malachi ii, 14; and نَّخْزِ St. Luke v, 7.

Line 3 :—

ᗝⳆⳑ ⳑⳑꝩ ɥⳑꝺɥꝩꭓ ꝼꝺꝩᖇ ɥꭓ ⳑⳑꝩ ꝺⳑꭓᗺ
ɥⳑꝺꝩꝳ ⳑⳑꝩᗺⳁ ᗗ ᗺꭓᗺ—ꝼ ᗗꝺꝳ ꝺꝳꝩɥ ɥꝺ
ꝼꝺⳑꝺ ⳑꝺꝩɥꝺ ᗗꭓ]ꝺ ~ ꝼꭓꝺɥᗺ ꝺꝺꝼⳑꝺ
ꝼꭓꝺ

From line 3 onwards we get sacrificial rules and details.

ꝺⳑꭓ. This is evidently the original of the later Hebrew אַלּוּף, an ox.

Psalm cxliv, 14.   אַלּוּפֵינוּ מְסֻבָּלִים
וַאֲנִי כְּבֶשׂ אַלּוּף

but פֶּרֶק and בָּקָר are more common Semitic. The ox stood *facile princeps* as a sacrificial animal among Semites.

Hindus and Egyptians worshipped him as a god, but Semites offered him to their God—Jehovah, Baal, Moloch, Ashtoreth, Chemosh.

The Phœnicians had three kinds of sacrifices, in all of which the 𐤀𐤔𐤋 figured, viz., the 𐤋𐤋𐤊, the 𐤓𐤏𐤍𐤕, and the 𐤔𐤋𐤌𐤋𐤋. We must first try to arrive at a conclusion as to the meaning of these words.

𐤋𐤋𐤊.* If we turn to the Hebrew Scriptures, we find that the word כָּלִיל is used; but not for a burnt offering like עוֹלָה; but as "a whole burnt offering" to be utterly burnt. Levit. vi, 23 (16 Hebrew text) כָּלִיל תִּהְיֶה לֹא תֵאָכֵל; also in the poetical passage in Deut. xxxiii, 10, it means "a whole burnt offering," וְכָלִיל עַל־מִזְבְּחֶךָ. It means the same in the Psalms as late as the age when Psalm li, 19, was written, עוֹלָה וְכָלִיל; but in the later books such as Ezekiel כָּלִיל means *perfection*, וּכְלִיל יֳפִי, Ezek. xxviii, 12, and in Syriac, the lineal descendant of the later Hebrew, it means "a garland" of beautiful flowers.

ܣܘܣܡܐ ܕܡܐܟܠ ܐܠܗܐ ܗܘ ܐܢ ܗܘ ܗܢܐ ܠܒܪ ܡܢ ܡܕܪܟܐ

Acts xiv, 12. ܐܢܫ ܠܥܠ ܗܘܐ ܣܩܠܝܢ ܠܒܓܝ ܘ ܪܝܕ.

These later words show clearly that the primal meaning of "totality" was lost in the full phrase, whole burnt offering. The Phœnicians took "burnt

* Note that in the Davis Carthago-tablet the word occurs in the plural 𐤋𐤋𐤊𐤌

offering" without "totality" and the Aramæic
Semites took "beauty" or perfect beauty as the
meaning, and dropped the idea of burnt offering.

The Phœnician 𐤑𐤅𐤏𐤕 does not occur in Hebrew,
Syriac or Arabic, in any root or derived form. We
are at a loss to get at its exact meaning; but as
𐤏𐤋𐤋 stands for עוֹלָה and 𐤔𐤋𐤌 𐤏𐤋𐤋 may fairly
be taken to represent something akin to the זבח
הַשְּׁלָמִים, then we must assume that 𐤑𐤅𐤏𐤕 is equal
to the אָשָׁם or the חַטָּאת.

The importance and frequency of the latter
causes us to accept חַטָּאת, 𐤑𐤅𐤏𐤕 then means the
offering which expiates the missing of the mark
through ignorance or negligence; but it may mean
זֶבַח לְפַלֵּא נֶדֶר, 𐤔𐤋𐤌 𐤏𐤋𐤋 as aforesaid is like
זֶבַח הַשְּׁלָמִים.

The order of the sacrifices with blood would then
agree in the main with the early simple code drawn
up by authority of Moses himself; for when the
Hebrew nomads were about to settle down as a
Syrian Semitic nation with Semitic neighbours,
Moses gave the nomads their law of the עוֹלָה,
זֶבַח לְפַלֵּא נֶדֶר, נְדָבָה, שְׁלָמִים and מִנְחָה, vide
Numbers xv. 3. 8.

Before passing on. it is only fair to say that it is
not absolutely certain that 𐤑𐤅𐤏𐤕 and 𐤔𐤋𐤌 𐤏𐤋𐤋
are distinct sacrifices.

𐤋𐤔𐤁𐤏𐤋 𐤋𐤌𐤒𐤃𐤔 𐤏𐤔𐤓. The Phœnician temple
dues in Marseilles included a gift of *money to*

the Temple priests, quite distinct from the mass of flesh retained for the Temple priests.

The Davis and Guienot inscriptions show that this practice was common in Carthage, that it was authoritative, though the sum is not detailed as in the Massilia-tablet. It only occurs once in the

Davis-tablet *in re* birds אבאצלו ‖ א ח נ צ ﬡ ﬡ

In the Guienot, generally נ צﬡﬡ ל ﬡ ﬡ ל.

The enormous amount of flesh retained by the College of Priests strikes one who lives in the East, for in the Holy Land, and on the plains of India, a bullock would not scale 300 pounds; but in Marseilles the priests could retain 300 pounds and still give back 300 pounds or more to the layman. The Davis-Carthago inscription does not give money to the priests in the greater sacrifices. It is therefore surprising that the Massilia sacrifice-tablet (coming from the Baal-city of Carthage) allows the European priests of Baal to take money instead of the skin, the feet, etc. *This is a non-Semitic custom.*

The priests of Semitic temples, from Jerusalem to Carthage, were paid in kind. Skins may have been very valuable in the Marseilles market, seeing that the laity gave ten shekels instead of one.

There cannot be the shadow of a doubt that the priests of Baal in Massilia were very well off with twenty-five shillings paid at every kind of greater sacrifice of a bullock and 300 pounds of flesh for every burnt offering of a bullock.

ﬡ ﬡ ﬡ ﬡ ﬡ ﬡ ﬡ ﬡ ﬡ ﬡ is good archaic Semitic for " over and above."

We find it in Job xvi, 14— יִפְרְצֵנִי פֶרֶץ עַל־

פְּנֵי פָרֶץ.

In the Decalogue it is the first phrase which strikes the eye: לֹא יִהְיֶה לְךָ אֱלֹהִים אֲחֵרִים עַל־פָּנָי, " other gods ranking over, above Me."

∼ must mean זֹאת just as אֲשֶׁר = ⱳ𝒳.

[𝑓𝒳𝑦𝑓ⱳ𝑳ⱳ * 𝑳𝒜𝑦ⱳ𝑦 𝒜𝒳]ⱳ is a restoration, but it is morally certain, as the layman is directed in line 6 to give 150 lbs. with a calf.

Line 4 :—

𝑦 𝑓𝒜𝑜𝒜𝑦𝑦𝑦 𝑓𝑳𝑦ⱳ𝑦𝑓𝒜𝑦𝑦 𝑓𝑜𝑦𝑦𝑔𝑦
𝑳𝑜𝑔𝑳 𝒜𝒳ⱳ𝒜 ⱳ𝒜𝕰𝒳𝑦 𝑦𝑦𝑜𝑦𝒜𝑦 𝑦𝑔𝑳ⱳ𝒜
𝕰𝑔∼𝒜

The 𝑓𝑜𝑦𝑦 was evidently distinct from the 𝑳𝑳𝑦.

Special portions of the body are in the 𝑓𝑜𝑦𝑦 given back to the layman; and special parts belong to the priests.

According to the Levitical Code for the worship of Jehovah, the priest who sacrificed the sin offering and the peace offering, took the fat parts, the kidneys, &c.. cut out the fat and burnt the fat to Jehovah, vide Leviticus viii, ix and x; and it is noticeable that the skin is mentioned there immediately afterwards, just as in the *Massilia*.

The prophets and priests who wrote the history of the sacrificial worship of Jehovah, and who represented Jehovah so anthropomorphically, tell us that

---

* 𝑳𝒜𝑦ⱳ𝑦 I translate freely as weight, taking it to equal מִשְׁקוֹל or מִשְׁקָל, but it may be a participial adjective.

the sweetest smell in the nostrils of Jehovah was the smell of the fat of kidneys. The fat was therefore cut off and burnt to Jehovah and the priests ate the flesh. This was always the case in the חַטָּאת, and so in the corresponding ⲡⲟⲩⲣ, the priest *cut out*, retained and ate the kidneys, etc.

ⲡⲁⲣⲯ must mean "parts cut out" with a secondary meaning added on.

ⲡⲗⲣⲧ is allied to אַצִּיל and אֵצֶל, the root-meaning of which is "*side*."

Ezekiel xiii, 18. עַל־כָּל אַצִּילֵי יָדַי,

Levit. xii, 12. אֵצֶל הַמִּזְבֵּחַ,

and may have been used in the sense in which we say "a side of mutton."

ⲡⲁⲟ עוֹר and ⲩⲩⲟⲡⲅ פְעָמִים are clearly "the skin and "the feet."

ⲩⲅⲗⲱⲅ looks like the entrails, bowels.

שִׁלֵּב means "to twine a border."

The ⲡⲁⲣⲯ and ⲡⲗⲣⲧ were הַשְׁלָבִּים, the perquisites of the priests.

The entrails, the feet and the *skin*, together with the rest of the flesh, were given back to the pious layman ⲉⲅⲛⲁⲗⲟⲅⲗ.

The word ⲗⲟⲅ must have had many shades of meaning; but it could not here mean the Hebrew "master," בַּעַל.

These details by their slight differences from the Levitical Code show us why the Jehovistic priestly

historians were so antipathetic to the priests of Baal.
The Baal-worship was so near and yet so far from
that of Jehovah. Just as two sisters who are
estranged are most bitter because of their knowledge
of each other.

The first grammatical point to note is the waw
conversive with the verb "to be," equalling "to
have."

ᗷᎩᐯᕱ ᒪᴏᎩᒪᎩᎩᎢ. And the lay offerer shall
have the skin, the feet, etc.

Ꭲ᙭ᙏᕱᐁᕱᎢᗷ᙭ is a good Semitic construct
clause.

ᎩᎩᒪᙏᕱ. It ought to be noted further that the
Davis and Guienot inscriptions, which were not so
carefully compiled, have ᎩᎩᒪᙏ᙭ᕱ.

On the assumption that Phœnician is near to the
Semitic mutter-sprache we should prefer our text.

אשלבים looks too Aramaic; but we remember
אֵין אֲטֹלל .

Line 5 :—

᙭ᎤᎩᎩᎤ᙭Ꭹ ᕱᎡ᙭ᗷᕱᎩᎡ Ꭹᒪ ᙙᎩᕱᙏ ᙡ᙭ ᒪᎲᎤᎡ
ᒪᒪᎩ Ꭹᒪᙡ Ꭹ᙭[ᖛᎤ]ᎩᎢᎩ᙭ ᒪᒪᎩ ᒪᙏ᙭Ꭱ Ꭹ᙭
ᒪᒪᎩ ᎡᎩ ᖻᗷ᙭Ꭱ ΙΙΙ]Ⅱ ᖛᙡᎩᗷᎡᎳᎡᎷ ᎩᎲᕱᎩᒪ
ᒪᎤ ᎩᒪᎲᎷᙏ

ᒪᎲᎤ, עֵגֶל, ﺣ݁ﺞﹶﻝ, ﻋﹺﺠﹾﻞ, are all good Semitic
for "a calf." As the phrase Ꭹᒪ ᙙᎩᕱᙏ ᙡ᙭ ᒪᎲᎤ

is good grammar for " a horned calf," then the suc-
ceeding phrases must be extra-descriptive.

‎𐤋𐤌 may be Phœnician for the old לִמוֹ of
Hebrew poetry; or it may agree with ‎𐤏𐤋𐤀 as
a collective. The collective taking the plural ‎𐤋𐤌.

‎𐤐𐤔𐤀𐤁𐤒 probably means in the state of still
lacking horns, or not yet fully formed, from חסר
" to lack aught."

Proverbs xxviii, 27. ‏נוֹתֵן לָרָשׁ אֵין מַחְסוֹר׃

St. Luke xii, 20. ‏نَفْسَكَ‎

‎𐤐𐤕𐤀𐤏𐤕𐤀𐤕 is almost impossible to explain as
a Semitic word. In its formation it goes against
all rules, turning the first and second radicals out of
place when re-duplicated ‎𐤕𐤀, ‎𐤕𐤀𐤕.

If we admit that the Phœnician traders knew
Greek, and, having picked up a little, transliterated*
the Greek into Phœnician characters, just as " the
Children of the Ghetto " do in London with their
scraps of German in their Yiddish, then we see at
once that this is probably the Phœnician patois for
ἄτμητος, viz.: ἀτομητος, not-castrated, = " a horned
calf, undeveloped, but not-castrated."

‎𐤀𐤕𐤋 𐤋𐤋𐤀 𐤕𐤀 𐤏𐤒𐤅𐤓[𐤕𐤀 𐤔𐤋𐤅 𐤋𐤋𐤀. What
kind of animal was the ‎𐤀𐤕𐤋? Its rules are

---

* μαχαιρα transliterated appears to be the only explanation of
‏מְכֵרֹתֵיהֶם‎, Genesis xlix, 5.

very carefully formulated. Was it a stag, אַיָּל, or a ram, אַיִל? A stag might well be paired with a calf as of equal weight and value.

It is good Phœnician usage for a deer to be offered to a *goddess*, but Baal is of the male sex. On the other hand the אַיִל, ram, is one of the commonest Semitic animals offerable as a sacrifice from the days of Abraham.

וַיֵּלֶךְ וַיִּקַּח אֶת־הָאַיִל וַיַּעֲלֵהוּ לְעֹלָה תַּחַת בְּנוֹ

Genesis xxii, 13.

We see this animal offered throughout the nomad forty years.*

לָקַח פַּר אֶחָד בֶּן־בָּקָר וְאֵילִם שְׁנַיִם

and in the later days of the Levitical Code the ram was specially laid down to be offered as an עֹלָה,

Levit. viii, 18. וַיַּקְרֵב אֵת אֵיל הָעֹלָה

The Massilia-tablet orders the same number of shekels to be paid with the 𐤀𐤉𐤋 and the 𐤏𐤋 viz., five—just half of what had to be given with the

---

* M. Clermont-Ganneau in his "L'Imagerie Phénicienne" says that the Massilia-tablet proves that the ram was in Carthage offered instead of a man, just as in the case of Abraham's offering. As Sayce points out, this coincidence between the sister religions of two Semitic nations can hardly be accidental. "Higher Criticism and the Monuments," page 186.

𐤀𐤋𐤉 and the priest retained for the sacred College just half the amount of flesh retained in the case of the 𐤀𐤋𐤉. The ram must also have been of greater size than now known to permit of the priests retaining 150 lbs. of meat, and yet of their being sufficient for the layman and his family (the family was the social unit). The skin of the ram does not appear to have been so valuable.

A hiatus occurs after the mention of the five shekels, and the *Corpus Inscriptionum* very properly inserts as in line 3, 𐤁𐤔𐤋𐤔𐤌 𐤄𐤊 𐤋𐤋𐤔 𐤌𐤔𐤔 𐤋𐤔 𐤏𐤋 for the next line begins with the 𐤐 of 𐤐𐤋𐤏.

As in the case of 𐤀𐤋𐤉 𐤋𐤋𐤉, the priest retained for the College the kidneys, caul, the side, etc., and gave back to the layman the skin, the feet, etc.

Line 6 :—

𐤐𐤔𐤔𐤁𐤄 ~ 𐤁𐤔𐤔𐤉𐤕 𐤔𐤔𐤀 𐤔 𐤔𐤔𐤔 𐤔𐤔𐤔𐤁𐤄 𐤌𐤔𐤐

IN 𐤄𐤔 ⟶ 𐤇𐤁𐤔𐤏𐤕 𐤏𐤔𐤀𐤕 𐤄𐤔𐤔𐤔𐤕 𐤇𐤔𐤌𐤔 𐤔𐤔𐤌

𐤄𐤔𐤁𐤕 𐤔𐤔𐤀𐤏𐤉𐤔 𐤄𐤔𐤔𐤔𐤔 𐤔𐤔𐤔𐤔

𐤄𐤔𐤔𐤉𐤔𐤔𐤄𐤋 𐤔𐤔𐤔𐤁

It is noticeable how many words are in common everyday use in Phœnician which are only just used in Hebrew. A Hebrew sacrifice-tablet would certainly have used בָּשָׂר instead of שְׁאָר, as in Levit. vii, 15, וּבְשַׂר זֶבַח תּוֹדַת שְׁלָמָיו. The Syriac also uses

〖ܡܐ〗.   The only printed type we can get of the
numerals is not much like those in the photograph.*
The restoration from 𝟺𝟺𝟶𝟽 onwards is certain.

The sacrifice-tablet now leaves well-known Semitic
words and lays down laws for other animals well
known, but with more obscure names.

Line 7 :—

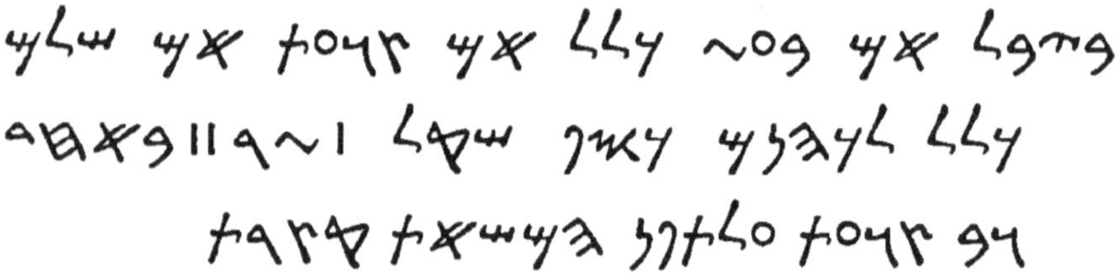

𝟺𝟦𝗐 𝟺𝐱 𝟊𝗈𝟦𝗋 𝟺𝐱 𝟦𝟦𝗒 ∿𝟶𝗀 𝟺𝐱 𝟦𝗀𝗍𝗀

𝟫𝐁𝐱𝟫‖𝟫∿�ǀ 𝟦𝗊𝗐 𝟽𝐱𝟦 𝟦𝟧𝟫𝟦𝟦 𝟦𝟦�›

𝟊𝟫𝗋𝟁 𝟊𝐱𝗐𝟦𝟥 𝟧𝟽𝟊𝟦𝟶 𝟊𝗈𝟦𝗋 𝟫𝟦

Line 8 :—

𝟦 𝟺𝟺𝟶𝟽𝟥𝟦 𝟺𝗀𝟦𝗐𝟥𝟦 𝟊𝟫𝟶𝟥 𝟧𝟦𝟦 𝟊𝟦𝗋𝗍𝟦

𝐁𝗀∿𝟥 𝟦𝗈𝗀𝟦 𝟫𝐱𝗐𝟥 𝗍 𝟫𝐁𝐱

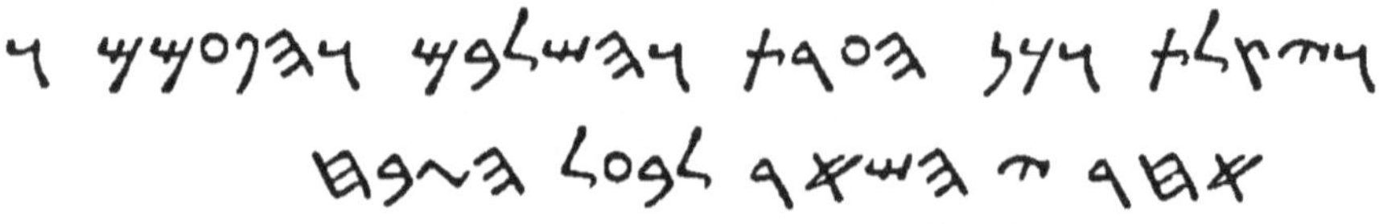

These two lines taken together lay down laws for
the 𝟦𝗀𝗍 and the ∿𝟶 which agree with the preceding laws, as the money payment of one and
three-quarter shekels is probably a proportionate
calculation.

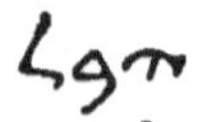

* This sentence was written before the fount of type used in
the present work was cast.—J. M. M.

𐤉𐤁𐤋 does not occur in Biblical or other Hebrew *as the name of an animal;* but the immediate connection of 𐤉𐤁𐤋 with 𐤏𐤆 which we know means a "she-goat," would lead us to suggest that 𐤉𐤁𐤋 means a he-goat. On the other hand יובל does occur in the Pentateuch in connection with festivals, joyful sounds, trumpets.

Joshua vi, 4, 6, שׁוֹפְרוֹת הַיּוֹבְלִים, may mean rams' horns or may mean sacred festival-trumpets.

A ram and a she-goat would be most unequally paired here in value, size, etc.

A ram and a calf is a far better pair, and here a he-goat and a she-goat.

If 𐤉𐤁𐤋 be not a he-goat, then the he-goat, which is such a common Semitic sacrificial victim, is absent from this Semitic sacrifice-tablet. To the present day the men of Islām sacrifice the he-goat. The بَکَرِی عِید is a great festival in India; its essence is the slaying of a goat. With reference to the money to be paid with the 𐤉𐤁𐤋 or with the 𐤏𐤆, the phrase 𐤆𐤓 𐤚 would be perplexing, were it not for the fact that the phrase is translated in line 11 רֶבַע שְׁלֹשֶׁת, so that its meaning is clearly three-quarters. Here the due paid is one and three-quarter shekels.

The sacred College still gets its 𐤒𐤑𐤓𐤕 and 𐤉𐤑𐤋𐤕, because it would be unprofessional to give back to the laity the parts whose fat has been a sweet savour in the nostrils of Baal, whether small parts or great. Note that in line 7 the word 𐤔𐤒𐤋 occurs *for the only time* in the Massilia-tablet, though it underlies the meaning of the price paid with every animal.

𐤔𐤒𐤋 does not occur in the Davis-Carthago-tablet. Line 8 is remarkably short, but there is no hiatus.

Line 9:—

[Phoenician inscription, three lines]

Line 10:—

[Phoenician inscription, three lines]

𐤀𐤌𐤓 is not a Hebrew word, but it is good Semitic for "a lamb."

Ezra vii, 17, Chaldee gives תּוֹרִין דִּכְרִין אִמְּרִין.

Ezra uses אִמְּרִין at about the date of the promulgation of the Massilia-tablet, two thousand miles away from the place where Artaxerxes' royal iradé was translated into Chaldee. Later on it is found in

St. Matt. vii, 15. ‎ܕܐܬܝܢ ܠܘܬܟܘܢ ܒܠܒܘܫܐ ܕܐܡܪܐ

Acts viii, 32. ‎ܐܝܟ ܐܡܪܐ ܠܢܟܣܬܐ ܐܬܕܒܪ

for *a sheep*.

✗⅃∧ resembles Hebrew. We have גְּדִי עִזִּים. and the plural גְּדָיֵי עִזִּים, in the historical books, and also in

Levit. iv, 23, שְׂעִיר עִזִּים

St. Matt. xxv, 32, ‎ܡܢ ܚܕܕܐ ܐܝܟ ܕܪܥܝܐ

⅃∽✗ ᠑∧⅃ is not a Hebrew conjunctive phrase for an animal; for the root meaning of the Hebrew צרב is "to burn"; but the context here shows that it means "youth." A lusty, fiery young ram may be the meaning evolved from צרב.*

‎ܡܣܪܗܒܐ means "hasty."

If errors in the Massilia sacrifice-tablet—a public authoritative document—be thought of for a moment, we might agree with Munk,† who says that it is an error for ᠑⅃᠑; vide ‎ܙܥܘܪ, small; but the Davis-Carthago-tablet also gives ᠑∧⅃. One of these tablets might have an error, but both could not be wrong.

---

* צרב is most probably the Aramaic ‎ܥܪܒܐ a *sheep* (like צֹאן ‎ܥ᠊). Note by Professor Driver.

† Munk, "L'Inscription Phénicienne de Marseille, 1847."

With these three young sacrificial animals the
pious layman gave three-quarters of a shekel to the
College, whether the sacrifice was ⌐⌐y, ⌐o⌐⌐ or
⌐⌐y y⌐⌐, and the priest also retained the kidneys,
etc.; but there is no notice of a large amount of flesh
being retained by the College.

The hiatus at the end of line 9 can easily be filled
up, for line 10 evidently begins with ⌐⌐⌐⌐o.

Note, that where the Massilia-tablet uses ⌐⌐y the
Davis-Carthago-tablet uses y⌐⌐y.

The Davis-Carthago here inserts

⌐⌐⌐ ⌐⌐ ⌐⌐⌐⌐ ⌐⌐ ⌐⌐⌐⌐ ⌐⌐ ⌐⌐⌐⌐⌐
⌐⌐ ⌐⌐⌐⌐⌐

but we shall treat of this later on, as the Massilia-
tablet has a similar direction in line 15.

Line 11:—

y⌐ [⌐]⌐y y⌐⌐ ⌐⌐ y⌐ ⌐⌐⌐⌐ ⌐⌐⌐[⌐]
⌐⌐⌐⌐ o⌐⌐ ⌐⌐ ⌐⌐⌐⌐⌐ ⌐⌐⌐ y⌐ ⌐⌐⌐
[·⌐⌐⌐⌐ ⌐o⌐⌐ ⌐⌐]⌐⌐ ⌐y ⌐ ⌐⌐⌐⌐⌐⌐⌐⌐

This line is the first portion of the inscription,
apart from the names in the first line, which shows
that it is a pagan tablet. Up to the present, I have
endeavoured to show the nearness of the laws of the

Baal-worship to those of the worship of Jehovah; and I have restrained myself from introducing Greek and Roman comparisons; but in line 11 we are introduced to *pagan augury* in a Semitic religious document. The hiatus in the first word is easily restored; the broken tail of the first letter shows that it is a ץ not a ס. It cannot be ריס. Restoring as above ריץ we now come to the sacrifice of *birds*.

This is similar to the order of sacrifices in Leviticus; where the pious Hebrew, if he could not bring a bullock or a ram for his אָשָׁם or חַטָּאת, he brought "two doves or two pigeons or the tenth part of an ephah of flour." Levit. xiv, 21, 22. צ∧ללל and צץ are both Semitic. If צ∧ללל be transliterated, it looks distinctly Aramæic אֲגֵן. The old Hebrew root-form גַּן means to protect.

2 Kings xix, 34. וְגַנּוֹתִי אֶל־הָעִיר

and the late author who writes in the decline of the nation even after the Restoration gives the Hiphil,

Zech. ix, 15. יָגֵן יְהוָֹה עֲלֵיהֶם

which gets us close to Aramæic:

Luke i, 35. ܘܚܝܠܗ ܕܡܪܝܡܐ ܢܓܢ ܥܠܝܟܝ

It probably means "barndoor" fowls here.

In opposition to barndoor fowls we have צץ, "game birds," which fly (from צִיץ). צץ luckily occurs in the Davis-Carthago, where the offerer pays the same as here.

Munk thought that ‏צץ‏ means "flowers." As a rule it is in the matter of this inscription "difficult to differ from" Munk; but I think that the slightest consideration of the end of the line should have convinced him that animals were meant; for the layman receives back (in both ‏אנלל‏ and ‏צץ‏) "the whole of the *flesh*."

It must be admitted that Munk has the general spirit of Hebrew on his side:

Isaiah xl, 6. ‏כְּצִיץ הַשָּׂדֶה‏
‏כְּצִיץ יָצָא‏

with only one or two exceptions, such as

Jerem. xlviii, 9. ‏תְּנוּ צִיץ לְמוֹאָב כִּי נָצֹא תֵצֵא‏

but the cumulative force of the sacrificial argument, the amount given, the flesh, etc., must weigh down the beam in favour of ‏צץ‏ as an animal.

A very striking point about the sacrifice of birds in Marseilles was that they could not be offered as a ‏עלל‏ or as a ‏צעות‏; they were offered as ‏עלל שלם שרא‏ or ‏בנת‏. Here we have the Semitic peace-offering conjoined with two pagan sacrifices. The inclusion of these in the national worship of Israel would be sufficient to explain the wrath of Jehovah against Baal-worship and the record of his hatred by his priestly historians.

שׁאן. The root-meaning of this is "overflowing," vide שׁצף and שׁטף, and a sacrifice with a meaning evolved from this root "a propitiatory sacrifice to avert the overflowing wrath of Baal." Halevy turns it "to avert calamity."* שׁסף has the idea of "minimizing calamity."

עוֹף. The idea of divination by watching the movements, the cries, the flight of birds, and of sacrificing in connection therewith is a practice which we associate with the Pagan Republic of Rome rather than with a Semitic nation; but as far as the *word* עוֹף is concerned it is essentially Semitic. We find חָזָה all through the Old Testament:

חֲזוֹן יְשַׁעְיָהוּ בֶן־אָמוֹץ אֲשֶׁר חָזָה

and the man, the seer, the prophet, is the חֹזֶה. We have God's seer, the king's seer, then we have the trusted holy men of Bel and Nebo,

הַחֹזִים בַּכּוֹכָבִים הַבְּרֵי שָׁמַיִם

but in these passages there is *not a word of watching birds.*

The Phœnicians may have picked up this startling addition to their sacrifices from the Romans; there would be Romans in Massilia, and the Baalic residents would respect Roman sacrifices.

As in the case of bullocks and rams, etc., a proportionate amount of money is given to the priests with each bird, viz., three-quarters of a shekel. From

* Halevy, "Nouvel Essai sur l'Inscription de Marseille."

the Davis-Carthago-tablet we see that though the Carthaginian worshipper followed the Semitic custom and gave the skin of the *bullock*, etc., to the priest without money, still the Carthaginian as well as the Massilian worshipper of Baal gave three-quarters of a shekel with each *bird*.

Line 12:—

(Phoenician inscription, three lines)

With regard to the hiatus at the beginning of line 12 I find myself unable to agree with the author of the monograph in the *Corpus Inscriptionum*. This painstaking scholar has assumed that the letter which still remains is an ⌐, and he has therefore fixed upon ⌐o as the word. The most cursory glance at the letter will show that it is an ⌐: it is as different from the initial ⌐ of 14, 16, 18, 20, and 21, as is chalk from cheese.

· Having assumed that ⌐o must be the word, he labours to get rid of the great difficulty of having two different articles next door to each other both treating of ⌐⌐⌐, the one introduced by ⌐ the other by ⌐o! The whole difficulty is an imaginary one. The preceding line (11) ends with ⌐⌐o and

12 begins with ᔇᔇ following the examples of 5 and 6, 9 and 10. Over and above the animal flesh, the layman was ordered to give a gerah (the twentieth part of a shekel) to the priests.

This corresponds with the order in line 6 :—

ᒪᕐᒍᗯᔭ ᕐᕽᗯ ·ᐱᖵᕽᗯᔭᕒ ᔇᔇᖵᒪᵒ

Such a thing as opposing my view to that of a great scholar is foreign to my nature; but I humbly submit my reading, because it makes no difficulties; and because it appears to follow examples.

ᖵᔭᕐᕒ is very Semitic, its rootmeaning being "early," then "first." The next word ᖵᗯᕐᕒ shows that the "holy firstfruits" are meant. This is a good example of words being good Hebrew words, but not expressing the Hebrew idiom. The Hebrew idiom is

Levit. ii, 14. מִנְחַת בִּכּוּרֶיךָ

In India we have thousands of examples of what is called "Babu English," good English words used by Indian clerks, but not making a good English idiom.

ᕐᕽᕒᕒᕒ would cause us at once to think of צoᵷ, צוּד, hunting. I suppose it must mean provision, etc., offered before going a hunting, or animals caught when hunting in the chase; but it seems curious that frankincense is left out of the sacrifices, particularly as oil, etc., are mentioned. With a High Altar and stone statues to various Baals there must have been frankincense.

C

The *Corpus Inscriptionum* gives ⟨glyph⟩ as corn, but I take ⟨glyph⟩ of line 14 to be corn. The Levitical code gives corn, oil, and frankincense :

גֶּרֶשׂ כַּרְמֶל וְנָתַתָּ עָלֶיהָ שֶׁמֶן וְשַׂמְתָּ עָלֶיהָ לְבוֹנָה

Levit. ii, 14.

There is a hiatus in the price.

The only letter remaining is ⟨glyph⟩. Ewald suggested ⟨glyph⟩, and the right-hand portion of the second (fragmentary) letter looks in the photograph like a ⟨glyph⟩. This would agree with אֲגוֹרָה in

1 Sam. ii, 36.   לְהִשְׁתַּחֲוֺת לוֹ לַאֲגוֹרַת כֶּסֶף

and with the commoner גֵּרָה :

Levit. xxvii, 25.   עֶשְׂרִים גֵּרָה יִהְיֶה הַשָּׁקֶל

The phrase ⟨glyphs⟩ looks ungrammatical, in fact incomprehensible, judged by ordinary rules of Semitic grammar; but two prepositions are not unknown in Phœnician epigraphy, such as ⟨glyphs⟩.

A hiatus now occurs of which we cannot fathom the meaning.

———

Line 13 :—

$$\text{שרׁׁ} \ \text{יולא} \ \text{ף}ׁ\text{)} \ \text{תאקׁyoם} \ \text{אׁ} \ \text{ף}o\text{ץ} \ \text{לׁ}[\text{9}]$$

$$\text{ף}o\text{ץגׁ} \ \text{ף}\text{לׁ}\text{ף}\text{יׁ} \ \text{ף}\text{אׁ}\text{ף} \ \text{ל}\text{)}\text{אׁ}\text{ל}$$

Following examples above, we may assert **9** at
the beginning of the line.

The line is not satisfying from the point of
view of conclusive argument; for we have by this
time come to the conclusion that ף o ץ 𐤓 is equal
to the חַטָּאת in the matter of sacrifices by blood;
but it is here mentioned after שׁלׁ and just before

9 לׁ 𐤀 .

The shorter Davis-Carthago inscription inserts this
notice after the sacrifices with blood; and before
the smaller sacrifices of the impecunious: in fact, just
before the ף 𐤀 לׁ y .

The Carthago arrangement is more natural; but
it may be that the ף o ץ 𐤓 is a general name or a
general sacrifice, which would be used in the
ף 𐤀 לׁ y just the same as in the sacrifices with
blood.

We must not be led away by Leviticus from the
fact that the Massilia-tablet is a sacrifice tablet of
Baal, and this a local, Western Baal.

y לׁ א ף 𐤔) in the plural may be explained by
the stone statues in 2 Kings x, 26.

אֵלִים in the plural, "gods," occurs in the national
pæan,

Exod. xv, 11.   מִי כָמֹכָה בָּאֵלִים

ל־פן agrees with *פ־ם* in showing that the genius of Phœnician does not require a preposition such as ‎ב. Hebrew does, e.g., לִפְנֵי הָאֱלֹהִים.

The Davis-Carthago tablet unaccountably gives *ב־ן־ם*, which is surely an error.

The Carthago tablet was not so carefully done by public authority as the Massilia.

ה־ם־ע־ש־ם is the Niphal, as in good Semitic, but עמס means "to load," not "to offer," as here.

Perhaps in Phœnician it developed into the meaning, "heaped up, laid before the gods."

2 Chron. x, 11. וְעַתָּה אָבִי הֶעְמִיס עֲלֵיכֶם עֹל כָּבֵד

I cannot offer any suggestion as to what follows the second *ר־ם־ע־פ*, for I could not have imagined the first which we have here.

Line 14 :—

ע־ל־ל־ב־ל־ע־ם־ב־ל־ע־ל־ל־י־ל־ב־א־ל־ם־ם־ש־ם־א־ג־ע

ל־[ר־ם־ע־פ־ש־א־ם־ע־ל־א־י־א־ש־א־ם־ו]

ל־[ם־ע־ש]־ם־ל

ל־ל־ב is an old Semitic form meaning "corn," Hebrew בְּלִיל.

The *Corpus Inscriptionum* takes it as equivalent to בְּלוּלָה, but the meaning is perfectly clear, as "corn" and בלולה ought to be *ל־ל־ב־פ*. Most critics have assumed that *ל־ם־ע־ל־ל־ב־ל־א ל־ם־ע* is a careless repetition, but there are two Semitic words with the same consonants :

חָלָב ‎حَلِيب‎ ܚܠܒ 𐤇𐤋𐤁 = milk.

חֵלֶב 𐤇𐤋𐤁 = fat.

Munk agrees that the Massilia-tablet deals with both fat and milk.

In a sacrifice-tablet, fat is a certainty; and, on the other hand, all Semitic tongues agree in representing milk by these consonants.

The Davis-Carthago inscription expresses the same idea in a simpler way, viz.,

𐤕𐤁𐤋𐤌𐤂 𐤁𐤂𐤔 𐤋𐤏

𐤁𐤂𐤔𐤋 𐤌𐤀𐤔 𐤔𐤀 𐤁𐤂𐤔 𐤋𐤊, is a curious phrase, we should have expected 𐤔𐤀 𐤔𐤀 אֲשֶׁר אִישׁ, but if it had been so written, commentators who object to

𐤇𐤋𐤁 𐤋𐤏𐤍 𐤇𐤋𐤁 𐤋𐤏 would certainly have said that 𐤔𐤀 𐤔𐤀 was a repetition.

𐤁𐤂𐤔𐤋 is the Semitic strong intention.

Genesis xv, 12. וַיְהִי הַשֶּׁמֶשׁ לָבוֹא

𐤕𐤁𐤋𐤌 is found throughout Semitic languages as an offering, very often as a "meal-offering," which is its meaning here, agreeing with

Levit. ii, 1. קָרְבַּן מִנְחָה לַיהוָֹה סֹלֶת יִהְיֶה
                                                    Hebrew.

Ezra vii, 17. וּמִנְחָתְהוֹן וְנִסְכֵּיהוֹן   *Chaldee.*

After the ⊟ of 𝑓⊟𝟝𝑦 there is a hiatus on the Massilia-tablet which would allow of three letters.

The writer in the *Corpus Inscriptionum* inserts the 𝑓 of 𝑓⊟𝟝𝑦, and then calmly passes on to the next letter found still and assumes that this is the ⊤ of 𝟝𝑦⊤; but in his printed reproduction of the photograph he leaves two spaces, one small and the other almost double. There is not the shadow of a doubt that some word of two or three letters came after 𝑓⊟𝟝𝑦 and before the w, as the *Corpus* assumes it to be.

After close examination I have satisfied myself that the letter is ∿, Hebrew 𝟋, and if we insert w𝑋 in the hiatus there remains space for one letter, and I suggest ∠ :

⊟𝟫∿∠ w𝑋

for there is a distinct remnant of an ∠ above the line. Then, after this, we could easily insert

𝑦𝟝𝟄𝑦∠ 𝟝𝑦⊤, etc., etc.

Line 15 :—

∠ᴀ 𝑦𝑋 𝑋𝟝𝟉𝑦 ∠ᴀ ⊟𝟫∿⊤ w𝑋 ⊟𝟫∿ ∠𝑦𝟫

—𝟝𝟄𝑦∠ 𝟝𝑦⊤ ∠𝟫 ᖱ𝟅𝟋

∠ᴀ is a good old Semitic word for "the poor." Its antithesis ᴀ𝟫𝑦 is often used with 𝑋𝟝𝟉𝑦 .

Genesis xiii, 2.   וְאַבְרָם כָּבֵד מְאֹד בַּמִּקְנֶה

𐤒𐤍𐤓 𐤋𐤀 appears to have been desperately poor.

𐤔𐤏𐤋 𐤋𐤁 is a peremptory prohibition; we therefore gather that the ecclesiastical authorities in the Baal-cult rigorously protected the poor.

The Davis-Carthago tablet has clearly 𐤉𐤂𐤋 in the singular and adds the grammatical form 𐤋𐤔𐤄 (מְנָה), compare the Syriac ܡܢܐ.

The idea of many critics that 𐤋𐤔𐤄 means the Greek μνα is too quaint.

Line 16:—

𐤋𐤀𝔵 𐤁𐤓𐤍𐤄 𐤋𐤄𐤍 𐤁𐤍𐤔 𐤋𐤄𐤍 𐤁𐤓𐤍𐤄 𐤋𐤄
—𐤁𐤓𐤍𐤕 𐤔𝔵 𐤄𐤄𐤀𝔵 𐤋𐤄𐤍

Munk thought that these were the names of other Phœnician sacrifices, but we have no 𐤁 at the beginning.

Renan thought that they represented classes of people in Carthage like the Roman equites, plebs. etc.*

זרח means "to rise," but אזרח was a person opposed to the גֵּר or מוֹלֶדֶת הוּץ. This makes for Renan's view. We may venture to translate 𐤁𐤓𐤍𐤄, "a son of the soil."

In the Old Testament 𐤔𐤐𐤄 was found only in the feminine שִׁפְחָה, "a maid-servant"; but the

* *Langues Semitiques.*

Phœnicians evidently used שׁבֿ for a slave of either sex.

א⅃אֿ בֿⁿqy is obscure, as meaning a person. In the Old Testament the root-idea is " feasting."

Amos vi, 7.   וְסָר מִרְזַח סְרוּחִים

Jerem. xvi, 5.   אַל תָּבוֹא בֵית מַרְזֵחַ is not so clear. Perhaps we may translate the clause "Every temple-servant who gives a feast."

⅃y אⁿⁿqא wא בֿqⁿ⌐ is quite grammatical; but, if the verb be singular, it would be more idiomatic if found *before* the plural noun. We know nothing of what followed בֿqⁿ⌐.

Line 17 :—

ſقⁿyy قবֿא বֿqⁿ ⌐o ſאⁿⁿy ſyন yⁿqאⁿন

[ſ]ſſⁿyſ ſⁿⁿ

From the presence of the Semitic ſyন, הֵמָּה, there must have been a verb just before yⁿqⁿא : perhaps ⌐qⁿⁿⁿ.

ſقⁿy is essentially a Phœnician phrase, often found with ⌐. The root-meaning is " to measure ": 1 Kings vii, 9.   כְּמִדּוֹת גָּזִית according to the ratio or measure.

ʄʍ probably means " laid down."

Ps. xlix, 14.　כַּצֹּאן לִשְׁאוֹל שַׁתּוּ

ʄɘʄɣɘ begins to talk about some well-known Book on Sacrificial Ceremonial.

Line 18 :—

> ɣʄɘɣ ·ᴎᴋʄɘ ʄʍ ᶫɘ ᴍᶍ ʍᶍ ʄᶍʍɥ ᶫ[ɣ]
> ᶫo ʍᶍ ɥʍᶍɘ ɘʄɣ ʍᶍ ʄɘʄɣɘ ᴍʄᶫ
> ɣʄᴇɘ ɘɘ ᶫoɘᴛᶫᴇ.ᴄ ʄo ʄʄᶍʍɥɘ

Line 19 :—

> ɣɘᴄɘᴇᴛ ɘɣʍᶍᴇɘ ɘɘ ᶫoɘᴛᶫᴇɣʄ

The missing letter in line 18 is a *ɣ* though a bad one. *ᶫɘᴍᶍ* is an extraordinary word.

We have already treated *ᶫɘ* as a powerful negative, but *ᴍᶍ* is an interrogative :

Genesis iv, 9.　אֵי הֶבֶל אָחִיךָ

Then how is the compound a simple negative? I suggest that it is a conditional possible negative, not probable, but *possible*.

ᴎᴋʄɘ must mean "in this tablet"; but it has no corresponding form in Hebrew.

ɣʄɘɣ. Hebrew would have led us astray; for we should by it translate " and they shall give"; but in Phœnician this would be 𐤀𐤔𐤓𐤋. The text must be Niphal with Waw Conv.

𐤋𐤏𐤓 is another peculiar Phœnician phrase, "according to," "following," like 𐤋𐤉𐤀𐤘 𐤘𐤀𐤉𐤋.

The Hebrew is עַל־פִּי.

There can be no manner of doubt that the writer in the *Corpus Inscriptionum* is correct in his restoration at the end of the line, according to the plan of lines 1 and 2; it so naturally agrees with line 19, which is fortunately preserved, and has the names running on continuously.

Line 20 :—

𐤔𐤔 𐤋𐤀𐤔𐤅 𐤑𐤓𐤀 𐤅𐤔𐤔𐤕 𐤇𐤈𐤉𐤕 𐤔𐤀 𐤋𐤀𐤏 𐤋𐤋
𐤋𐤒𐤋𐤔𐤅— 𐤔𐤀𐤉𐤓𐤀𐤐

This is an authoritative warning to rapacious priests.

𐤑𐤓𐤀 as it stands is unintelligible. It may be an error for 𐤑𐤓𐤀, though this is an assumption from which I shrink in connection with an authoritative public document and particularly in a clause warning the Temple priests. If it ought to be 𐤑𐤓𐤀 then we endeavour to interpret it along the plane of רוץ to "run over the brim" or "to stretch out" as in

Psalm lxviii, 32.   כּוּשׁ תָּרִיץ יָדָיו לֵאלֹהִים

any priest *overstretching* the limit of the Temple dues

is to be severely fined; but we have unfortunately lost the record of the amount both in the Massilia and Carthago-tablets. This is most annoying.

ﺵﻳﻭﻝ "shall be fined" is the Niphal with Waw Conversive. This Niphal is clearly seen in

עָנוֹשׁ יֵעָנֵשׁ כַּאֲשֶׁר יָשִׁית עָלָיו בַּעַל הָאִשָּׁה

Exod. xxi, 22.

Line 21 :—

ﺍﻟﻜﺘﺎﺑﺔ ﺍﻟﻔﻴﻨﻴﻘﻴﺔ

The first letter of the line looks rather like a ﻝ, but as in line 18 we take the liberty of considering the word to be ﻝﻳ.

ﺕﻛ . The sign of the accusative is interesting. The hiatus in the centre of the line cannot be composed of a single word and the word beginning with ﻳ shows no sign of an ﻝ, so I prefer ﺟﻛﻳ, and as the last of the five letters shows by its remnant that it is a ﺕ, I venture humbly to suggest the reduplication of the former ﺕﻛ and to restore the authoritative warning to rich niggardly laymen.

As regards the date of publication of the tablet, I think it very probable that Massilia was one of the colonies founded by Hanno at the close of the sixth century before Christ, in order to get rid of the half-breeds and slaves, who, now freed from slavery, were becoming too powerful in Carthage. The tablet would go with the settlers and the merchants or would be sent shortly afterwards.

As the date of publication in the fifth or sixth century B.C. is not a very important matter, I have merely mentioned it here at the end of the thesis. The character shows that it could not be later than the fifth century, i.e., about the time of Ezra's return from Babylon.

Quite a number of thoughtful clergy and lay friends interested in the monuments have asked me to publish an English edition of the Massilia sacrifice-tablet. Of course all Semitic scholars have seen the Latin edition in the *Corpus Inscriptionum*, but in their books they merely refer to the the tablet as in existence in Marseilles. Rawlinson notes the fact in his "History of Phœnicia": so does Sayce in his "Higher Criticism and The Monuments": but it is high time that the Carthaginians should be allowed to speak for themselves in English about their religion, or about any of its details, when a well-known book of reference like "Chambers' Encyclopædia" publishes an article on *Carthage*, wherein the writer says that "the Carthaginians had no order of priests"! The crass ignorance of such a statement can only be dispelled by the publication of such theses as the Massilia-Carthago; for *the Massilia-tablet mentions the priests ten times in twenty-one lines.*

The Carthago-tablet follows the Massilia in using both "priests" and "priest," and mentions them six times in eleven fragmentary lines. The Guienot tablet uses "priest" only. All three tablets were graven and published in Carthage itself by Government authority, though the Massilia one was more carefully done. It is popularly believed, on the authority of Roman writers, who were enemies of Carthage, that the Carthaginian religion was simply the worship of fire and especially by human sacrifice.

The Massilia-tablet shows that this is as true as the Christian belief that none could with safety go near the procession of the Jagannath (Juggernauth) car. During the present *century* there have been no persons pushed under the wheels of Jagannath's car, and only three instances of people throwing themselves under the car! In like manner it will be seen from the Massilia-tablet that *the ordinary worship of Baal in Carthage or Massilia did not include human sacrifice.*

The preparation of this thesis has been an engrossing labour of love, begun in England, continued in France, and now finished in India.

If, by an English annotated edition of the Massilia-tablet, I could bring some slight confirmation of the truth of Leviticus as a Semitic code to the large number of English students of the history of the Bible, who prefer English books on any subject, it would be a great pleasure to me to publish it, even though these same earnest students of the Old Testament in English should be shocked at first to find so much in common between a *pagan* sacrifice-tablet and the sacrificial code of the chosen people of Jehovah.

www.ingramcontent.com/pod-product-compliance
Lightning Source LLC
Chambersburg PA
CBHW021432090426
42739CB00009B/1461